# Jake's

Story by Annette Smith
Photography by Lindsay Edwards



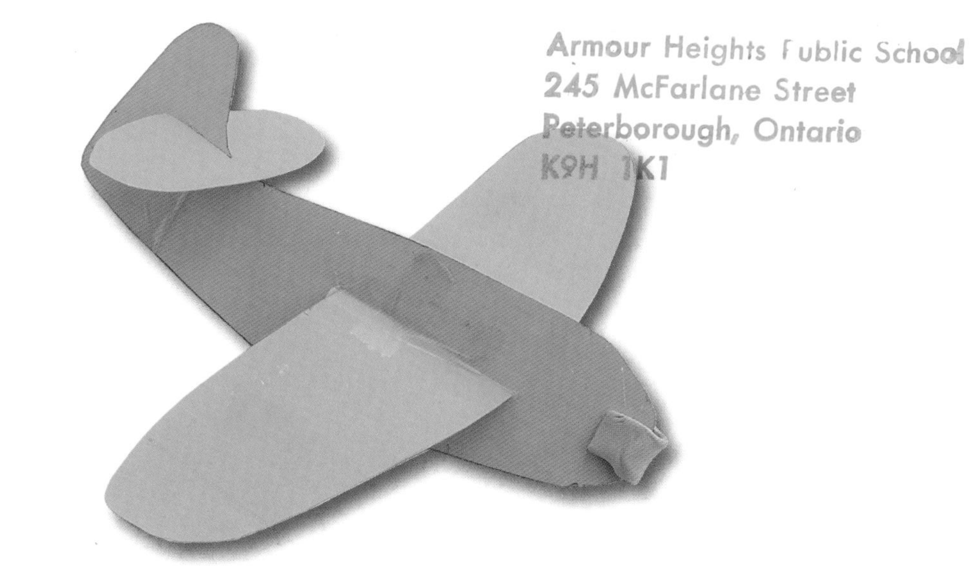

"I like this book, Dad,"
said Jake.
"Look at this big plane."

Market in the dark over Axa
Odd views from the moral high ground

"Can you get me a toy plane
like this, please, Dad?"
said Jake.

"Not today," said Dad.

Aircraft — machines that fly
space shuttle

"I will **make** a plane," said Jake.
"I will make it
out of this green card."

Market in the dark over Axa

Jake cut out his plane.

And he cut out the tail.

"The tail goes in here," he said.

Jake cut out the wings.

"Dad, I can not get the wings
to stay on," he said.

Dad looked at Jake's plane.

"The wings go in here,
like this," said Dad.

"This will help your plane
to fly, too," he said.
"It goes here on the nose."

"Thanks for helping me, Dad,"

said Jake.

"Come and fly your plane outside,"

said Dad.

"Look at my plane!" shouted Jake.
"It is going way up in the sky."